POP PEOPLE™

98°

By Eartha Glass

POPPEOPLE™

98°

By Eartha Glass

SCHOLASTIC INC.

New York   Toronto   London   Auckland   Sydney   Mexico City   New Delhi   Hong Kong

WHAT'S INSIDE

POPPEOPLE™

98°

By Eartha Glass

iNTRODUCTiON

Has your CD player been working overtime since 98° released *Revelation*? The quartet's fourth album is brimming with sweet ballads and gonna-get-you-groovin' tracks that fans *cannot* get enough of!

Jeff Timmons, Justin Jeffre, Drew Lachey, and Nick Lachey know how to turn up the heat. The first two singles from *Revelation,* "Give Me Just One Night (*Una Noche*)" and "My Everything," burned up the airwaves the minute the album dropped, back in late September 2000.

One listen to *Revelation* proves that 98° is movin' on up as a singing group. The album marks a new era. The guys are still crooning their trademark love ballads, but there are also some funky up-tempo flavors to their sound this time around. According to Universal

Records, 98°'s record label, "The group is destined to keep on inspiring people." No kidding!

Don't fret if *Revelation* wasn't on your holiday or birthday wish lists. It's not too late. Just get to your nearest record store and pick up a copy. *Revelation* is still very much on the hip-tip and is spawning hit after hit.

If you've had your copy of *Revelation* for a good while now and know all the words to the latest tunes from 98°, then get ready to prove it. You can sing along with Drew, Justin, Jeff, and Nick live in concert when they come to your area. The 98° *Revelation* tour kicked off in late 2000 and is carrying on well into 2001. You can bet these hunks are setting hearts afire across the globe. Have you gotten your concert tickets yet? Don't miss out on the *Revelation* revolution!

Chapter 1

Secrets 'N' Stuff

When Justin, Drew, Nick, and Jeff headed into the studio back in 2000 to record their fourth album, they had a tough act to follow — their own! Their previous studio album, *98° And Rising,* went multiplatinum (selling about five million copies) and spawned the top-ten hits "Because of You," "The Hardest Thing," and "I Do (Cherish You)."

There was a lot of pressure on the guys. Maybe some bands would have stalled and had a tough time of it, but not 98°. They *groove* when the heat is on!

Before going into the studio, the guys took a well-earned break. They rang in the new millennium and then headed off in various directions for mini vacations: Justin flew to the Caribbean; Drew went to Mexico; Jeff kicked back in Southern Cali; and Nick hung out with his girlfriend, Jessica Simpson, who was on the road. (More dish on that later on!)

But music is always close to their souls no matter where they are or what they're doing. Even as they were taking a break they were thinking about their next album.

Instead of focusing on trying to top *98° And Rising*, however, Jeff, Drew, Nick, and Justin decided on a totally new approach. From the start, they've followed what's in their hearts, and this time, their hearts told them to take a chance and try something different.

And they decided to go for it.

"We feel like we've proven what we can do with a ballad," Drew told *Billboard* Online. "Our goal this time was to show more versatility in our music."

So with lyrics and riffs bubbling and brewing inside their heads, they started penning some new songs. By spring 2000, they were ready to head into the studio and start laying down the tracks.

The band recorded all the songs in one city — Los Angeles, California — and worked with a variety of producers. Since they had such a great time working with Anders Bagge and Arnthor Birgisson (the duo who produced their holiday album, *This Christmas*, as well as their top-three smash, "Because of You"), the guys decided to stick with them on *Revelation*.

Working with a bunch of talented producers lent a unique sound to each song. By the end of every session, the quartet was that much closer to fulfilling their dream of venturing into new musical territory.

Special Secrets

So, how exactly is an album made? Some musicians follow a formula: They write all the songs first, they record them one after the other, and then the record company packages and ships the album off to record stores.

With *Revelation*, Nick, Jeff, Drew, and Justin did things their own way. They ended up stirring a little bit of everything into the mix. Even as they were laying down tracks, they were still perfecting lyrics and getting in sync with the soul of each song. Lots of times, songs "come together" in the studio, and it's important for a singer or group to keep an open mind. Of course, the guys were hip to this and knew that if they really wanted to reach a new horizon with the album, they'd have to let the songs come alive and lead *them*. Bottom line — Drew, Justin, Jeff, and Nick had to keep the faith and trust one another and their producers.

In between recording songs, they were thinking about a whole lot of other questions: Which song should be the first single? What should the video be like? What would be the coolest shot for the cover of the CD?

Way before the last track was recorded, the guys were doing photo shoots for the album, checking out artwork and liner notes, and last but most definitely not least, trying to come up with a title for the album.

98° thought long and hard about that perfect title. It wasn't easy, considering all the new ground they were breaking musically for themselves.

Back in 1995 when they had just formed, the guys were in a similar situation, figuring out a name for the band. Before Drew joined, Jeff, Nick, and Justin were performing at talent shows under the name Just Us with Jon.

After Jon quit Just Us to pursue acting, and Drew joined up, obviously that name didn't fit anymore. Other names they tossed around were Next Issue, Inertia, and Verse Four. Then they happened on 98° — and something clicked. It nailed the vibe and groove of their songs — passionate, heartfelt, and hot, hot, hot.

Everything 98° does, they do together. And choosing the title of their fourth disc was no different. They threw out a bunch of names until one day someone came up with *Revelation*. It was perfect! Why? Because this album was something new for the group, and with it they would be unveiling a new side of themselves to the world with songs *they* wrote. And that is what a "revelation" is — a sort of unveiling.

By the start of summer 2000, the band had finished recording *Revelation*. Their studio time clocked in at a whopping 90 days — considered to be a *lot* of time. Of course, it's taken other musicians much longer to finish an album, but the guys' experience was an intense one, filled with long hours and hard, hard work. Their dedication paid off in the end, big time.

While the songs on *Revelation* were being mixed and mastered, the guys were getting psyched for the release of the first single, "Give Me Just One Night (*Una Noche*)" and finalizing plans for the video shoot. In between, days were filled with press interviews, updating their official Web site, hopping into a series of online chat rooms to hang with their fans, working out and doing photo sessions for oodles of teen 'zine and music mag covers.

Now that they've taken their smooth 'n' sweet love songs to the next level, is 98° satisfied with what they've achieved on *Revelation*?

"Whether our sales are booming or not, we'll be proud of what we've done in the studio," Justin told *YM* magazine.

Chapter 2

Dazzling *Revelation*

Tracks on *Revelation*

"Give Me Just One Night (*Una Noche*)"

"The Way You Want Me To"

"Stay the Night"

"Yesterday's Letter"

"He'll Never Be (What I Used to Be to You)"

"I'll Give It All" (Interlude)

"My Everything"

"You Should Be Mine"

"You Don't Know"

"Dizzy"

"The Way You Do"

"Always You & I"

"Never Giving Up"

Bonus Tracks

"Can You Imagine" (only at Wal-Mart)
"The Only Thing That Matters" (only at Target)
"Chance to Love You More" (only at K-mart)

The Deal on "Give Me Just One Night (*Una Noche*)"

Swedish producing sensations Anders Bagge and Arn-thor Birgisson penned a song titled "Give Me Just One Night (*Una Noche*)." Originally, the duo had imagined Ricky Martin singing it, but then they decided it would really be great for 98°. With a little tweaking, it was a perfect fit for Jeff (first tenor), Nick (second tenor), Drew (baritone), and Justin (bass). The hot percussions and Spanish guitars of the Latin-flavored love song added a spicy twist to the band's sound.

If you don't speak Spanish, you may have been a little confused when "Give Me Just One Night (*Una Noche*)" first came out. The album hadn't yet been released, and some fans were nervous that the guys had swapped thier awesome ballads for a Latin-flavored sound.

During an online interview, Justin was up at bat

when a fan asked him what the deal was with the Spanish-type music.

"That's the only hint of Spanish on the album," said Justin. "We just like it because it felt good. We've been inspired by all different types of music, including Latin music."

"Dizzy"

The guys could have stopped there, but they continued exploring and soon ended up having a little fun with rap. The track "Dizzy" offers a fun-'n'-funky rap, courtesy of Nick. It was a spur of the moment thing. "That was kind of an experiment on the demo," Nick explained during the *Revelation* press tour.

Turned out Nick's little rap stuck, and the group dug the new corner their music had turned. Nick's a total natural when it comes to rhyming, but he's said it's unlikely that rap would become a main focus of the group anytime in the near future.

How come?

Sing Me a Love Song!

'Cause if there's one thing that put 98° on the map, it's their smoochy love songs. The quartet's smooth crooning had girls swooning lickety-split. Cases in point: "I Do (Cherish You)," "Still," and "The Hardest Thing."

Jeff, Nick, Drew, and Justin are all over those. Not only because those red-hot ballads fanned the flames for the group not so long ago, but simply because these four sweeties always have been and always will be romantics. They just love singing 98° style — straight from the heart.

So that's why *Revelation* is chock-full of classic 98° love songs. "My Everything" is a real heart-melter; "Always You & I" is full of hope and faith; and "Yesterday's Letter" brings tears to many fans' eyes. As Drew puts it, short and sweet, "Harmony is our thing."

About *Revelation* in Their Own Words

Justin's favorite *Revelation* track:

"I guess my favorite song is 'My Everything.' I got to help write it, and I just think it's a song that feels good. It's got beautiful lyrics." [Online chat room]

Nick on his girlfriend Jessica Simpson inspiring "My Everything":

"That song is purely dedicated to her and she knows that." [Universal Records]

Drew's favorite *Revelation* song to perform:

"It changes regularly, but right now my favorite would be "The Way You Want Me To." [Online chat room]

Jeff on one of the reasons *Revelation* has more danceable tracks:

"Every time we go to a club, we never hear any of our stuff because it's too slow. So we wanted to make some music that would get people out of their seats." [Online interview]

Take a Temperature Reading

Do you have a career ahead of you as a music critic? According to you, what are the temperature readings on each of these songs from the *Revelation* album? After rating each song, try to write a few words telling what strikes you about the lyrics and/or music and how the song makes you feel. Check out the list of words below to get those creative juices flowing.

88° = On the cool tip
98° = Right on the nose
99° + = Burnin' it up, baby!

Here are some words to help get your reviews going:

Awesome   Jammin'   Scorching
Blazing   Kind   Tender
Cherish   Lovable   Up-tempo
Deep   Marvelous   Very very
Excellent   Nice   Warm
Fiery   Outta sight   eXceptional
Gorgeous   Pure   Yearning
Handsome   Quiet   Zippy
Intense   Rhythm

"Give Me Just One Night (Una Noche)"
    I rate it_____
    Because_____

"The Way You Want Me To"
    I rate it_____
    Because_____

"Stay the Night"
    I rate it_____
    Because_____

"Yesterday's Letter"
    I rate it_____
    Because_____

"He'll Never Be (What I Used to Be to You)"
     I rate it_____
     Because_____

"I'll Give It All" (Interlude)
     I rate it_____
     Because_____

"My Everything"
     I rate it_____
     Because_____

"You Should Be Mine"
     I rate it_____
     Because_____

"You Don't Know"
     I rate it_____
     Because_____

"Dizzy"
     I rate it_____
     Because_____

"The Way You Do"
     I rate it_____
     Because_____

"Always You & I"

I rate it_____

Because_____

"Never Giving Up"

I rate it_____

Because_____

Chapter 3

Sizzling Climb Year By Year

Though Justin, Jeff, Nick, and Drew all hail from Ohio, that's not where 98° was born. Jeff was living in Los Angeles when he was trying to put together a singing group. A lot of people tried out, but things didn't click till he hooked up with Nick. At the time, Nick was in college, studying sports medicine. But when he got the call from Jeff, he was thrilled. The two guys sang to each other over the phone to see if their voices jibed — happily, they did! Nick then suggested his high school buddy Justin who sang a mean bass, and his own little bro, Drew, who could definitely kick the baritone. Once Drew and Justin signed up, their fab four-part harmonies were complete, and 98° exploded on the music scene in 1995.

1995: Nick, Jeff, Drew, and Justin perform at the House of Blues in Los Angeles, California. The guys make ends meet by doing all sorts of odd jobs, including working as security guards (Justin and Jeff), delivering Chinese food (Nick), and working at a deli (Drew).

1996: The guys score a deal with Motown Records and begin working on their first studio album.

1997: Their self-titled debut album, *98°*, is released on July 29. "Invisible Man" burns its way up the charts. The guys start touring and begin attracting more and more fans.

1998: The debut album *98°* is reissued on March 10 with a new ballad. The second album, *98° And Rising*, is released October 27 and spawns hit after hit.

1999: The group signs with Universal Records and releases *This Christmas* on October 19. The guys continue performing and making special appearances.

2000: The band's much-awaited fourth album, *Revelation*, is released on September 26. They turn up the heat by performing on the morning and late-night talk-show circuits as well as on prime-time TV by singing on the sitcom *Just Shoot Me*. They also jump into the new millennium with two new managers. In December, the *Revelation* tour kicks off.

2001: After the conclusion of their *Revelation* tour, the guys head back into the studio and begin working on their *fifth* album. Can't wait!

Chapter 4

is it Hot in Here or What?!

JEFF
Full Name: Jeffrey Brandon Timmons
Vocal Part: First tenor
Birthday: April 30, 1973
Birthplace: Canton, Ohio
Grew Up: Massillon, Ohio
Height: 5'8"
Weight: 160 lbs.
Hair: Brown
Eyes: Blue
Parents: Patricia and James
Birth Sign: Taurus
Nickname: Sugar
Fave Colors: Orange, blue
Fave Actor: Robert DeNiro
Fave Actress: Salma Hayek

Fave Foods: Denny's breakfasts; steak and seafood
Duet Fantasy: With Babyface

NICK
Full Name: Nicholas Scott Lachey
Vocal Part: Second tenor
Birthday: November 9, 1973
Birthplace: Harlan, Kentucky
Grew Up: Cincinnati, Ohio
Height: 5'10"
Weight: 180 lbs.
Hair: Brown
Eyes: Blue
Parents: Cate and John
Birth Sign: Scorpio
Nicknames: Hollywood, Slider
Fave Color: Red
Fave Actor: Bruce Willis
Fave Actress: Michelle Pfeiffer
Fave Foods: Skyline chili, pretzels, ice cream, steak
Duet Fantasy: With Sade

JUSTIN
Full Name: Justin Paul Jeffre
Vocal Part: Bass
Birthday: February 25, 1973

Birthplace: Mount Clemens, Michigan
Grew Up: Cincinnati, Ohio
Height: 5'10"
Weight: 150 lbs.
Hair: Brown (sometimes blond!)
Eyes: Blue
Parents: Sue and Dan
Birth Sign: Pisces
Nicknames: Droopy, Hydro, Big J
Fave Color: Blue
Fave Actor: Robert DeNiro
Fave Actress: Reese Witherspoon
Fave Foods: Pizza, donuts, Skyline chili
Duet Fantasy: With Mariah Carey

DREW
Full Name: Andrew John Lachey
Vocal Part: Baritone
Birthday: August 8, 1976
Birthplace: Cincinnati, Ohio
Grew Up: Cincinnati, Ohio
Height: 5'6"
Weight: 148 lbs.
Hair: Brown
Eyes: Hazel
Parents: Cate and John

Birth Sign: Leo
Nickname: Sprout
Fave Color: Navy blue
Fave Actors: Mel Gibson, Harrison Ford
Fave Actress: Rene Russo
Fave Foods: Pizza, donuts, and lots of junk food
Duet Fantasy: With Shania Twain

As a fan of 98°, you're special, too. The guys think their fans are the best 'cause they're so totally devoted. Jeff once said of 98° fans, "We're surprised and thrilled that they are so dedicated to us." So add your personal info below, and see how much you have in common with these Ohio honeys!

Full Name: _____

Birthday: _____

Birthplace: _____

Grew Up: _____

Height: _____

Weight: _____

Hair: _____

Eyes: _____

Parents: _____

Birth Sign: _____

Nickname: _____

Fave Color: _____

Fave Actor: _____

Fave Actress: _____

Fave Foods: _____

Duet Fantasy: _____

Fave 98° Member: _____

Fave 98° Songs: _____

Fave 98° Videos: _____

Chapter 5

Girl Talk

If you know anything at all about 98°, it's probably the fact that these guys are total Romeos at heart. They love to sing about love, write about love, and *be* in love. Here's how Drew, Justin, Nick, and Jeff are romantic in their unique ways.

Justin

Justin likes being with a girl he doesn't have to impress, though he does admit to having written a song for a special someone. It was the first one he ever wrote.

Definitely the sensitive type, Justin makes a point of writing his thoughts in his journal. If he needs to think deep thoughts, he usually does so by himself in a quiet place. Sometimes he reads a book or listens to a favorite CD.

Do you put on your favorite 98° songs when you need to think about life?

Though he finds girls difficult to understand sometimes, Justin still loves them. Staying true to himself is very important to him, and he's not the type of guy who puts on airs. In fact, he still gets a little nervous around a girl he digs. Ultimately, this Pisces hunk wants someone who will love him for himself.

A romantic date with Justin might start with him picking a girl up in his truck and taking her out to a nice place to eat. After that, maybe they'd head over to a cool jazz club. He doesn't mind a little salsa music now and then, either.

Currently, Justin is unattached. Life on the road is hard on relationships, and Justin has said that being single at this point in his life has its pluses.

Still, he would love to have a girlfriend to share his life with. A girl who's mellow but has a strong sense of self would catch his eye.

Nick

Nick is currently dating singer Jessica Simpson. (Most fans already knew that.) They first met at a holiday parade when they had the same manager. Nick and Jessica hit it off immediately. They liked each other a lot, but they still took things slowly. Nick believes that in order to genuinely love someone, you've got to get to know the person inside and out. And they've also got to get to know you. Once these two became good friends, love quickly blossomed. Every January 10 marks another anniversary for these lovebirds.

In general, Nick likes a girl who definitely knows what she wants and also knows how to laugh when times are tough. "Headstrong" is the adjective he's used to describe his girl type.

When Nick is really taken with a girl, he's the type of guy who gets swept up with emotion. One time, he took his mother's car without permission and drove to a gal pal's house. Parting is such sweet sorrow, and poor Nick just couldn't bear to be apart from his sweetheart. He was grounded (of course).

Well, that's how Nick gets swept off his feet, but this sweetie does a little sweeping of his own. For instance, the song "My Everything" was written with Jessica in mind. Nick loves pouring out his feelings via those 98° ballads.

He also considers himself to be the most romantic of the bunch (Jeff, Justin, and Drew would beg to differ). Fittingly, Nick's favorite color is red.

Nick might begin to woo his date by giving her a

dozen red roses. A candlelit steak dinner might be next. He's just as at home at a barbecue, drinking Yoo-hoo. But no radishes, beets, or liver, please.

Nick believes communication is very important in a relationship. He enjoys kicking back and chatting. He's not one to shy away from deep conversations and likes a girl to speak her mind.

As much as Nick likes action-packed films like *Die Hard*, he also has a soft spot for romantic films, or what some people like to call "chick flicks." His fave chick flicks are *Steel Magnolias* and the romantic classic, *Gone With the Wind*.

When he's missing Jessica and he can't be with her or get her on the phone, Nick sometimes visits her Web site and gazes into her eyes onscreen. Ahhh, what a sweetie. . . .

Drew

No one would ever guess Drew is younger than the other guys in 98°. It's never been an issue because the guys treat one another with respect regardless of their age. In fact, Nick has said in the past that the rest of the group look to Drew for guidance.

The guys do sometimes call sensible Drew by his nickname, Sprout. But they do it with a lot of love. One thing they would never call him, however, is "Andy." Drew has never liked that nickname. He's always been called Drew.

Sensible as the other guys say he is, Drew is occasionally a spur-of-the-moment kind of guy. He once drove 1300 miles to surprise a girl he liked when he had a few days off. Of course, she was shocked when she saw Drew drive up.

Another Drew surprise came last October when news broke that the 98° dreamboat had gotten married. Drew proposed to his longtime girlfriend, Lea Dellecave, and the two tied the knot last autumn in their hometown of Cincinnati.

To friends and family, the wedding came as *no* surprise as the lovebirds have a mega long history. Drew and Lea have been best buds since the age of nine. They both attended Cincinnati's School for the Creative and Performing Arts. Before Drew popped the big question, the two had been dating for more than seven years. You can bet the wedding was as dreamy as dreamy can be — right out of a fairy tale!

Since that special day, the newlyweds have been inseparable. In fact, Lea, who is an awesome choreographer and dancer, appeared onstage with 98° during their *Revelation* tour.

Though you'd never know it watching him shake it on stage, Drew says dancing is not really his thing. But with a little help from Lea, he's gotten used to it. Rather than sweating it out at a dance club, though, Drew works up a sweat by exploring the great outdoors and going camping.

When he was 16, Drew was a counselor at an outdoor camp for inner-city youth. The experience made him realize that he wanted to help others who are less fortunate than he is.

That's one of the reasons Drew took a job in New York City as a paramedic. Another reason was that this rugged cutie likes a good dose of adventure in his life. The Big Apple dishes out plenty of that! Drew is definitely at home with the excitement big city life has to offer. (FYI: Brother Nick finds New York City a little too big and fast-paced and wouldn't want to call it home.) Drew was totally psyched when the guys were invited to take part in the Christmas tree lighting in New York's Rockefeller Center in the 2000 holiday season 'cause he got to catch up with his New York buddies and visit some of his old hangouts.

In the past, Drew has described himself as an extremist. Skydiving and bungee jumping, which are things he'd like to do, are pretty extreme!

Still, Drew is a Midwestern boy at heart and enjoys the slower-paced life of Cincinnati. He loves hanging out with his friends and kicking back at a local football game.

Drew has a soft spot for the *Revelation* track "The Way You Do," which expresses how great and powerful a force love can be.

Jeff

Jeff has a longtime girlfriend whom he loves very much. Though being on the road is sometimes hard on the relationship, he also feels it puts things into perspective. The couple appreciate every minute they get to spend together and with their little daughter, Alyssa.

Being humble comes naturally to Jeff. He insists on treating everyone with respect, and people he likes are also considerate in that way.

Jeff may be taken, but he does have some advice for girls who have their eye on a certain boy. He believes being yourself speaks volumes over how your hair looks or what kind of jeans you wear. Jeff is a solid guy who knows what makes him happy, and he wants his fans to know being true to yourself is the only way to go.

When he has free time, Jeff checks out the Dallas Cowboys (his favorite team). For a fun time out with his little family, Jeff might go to Denny's (he loves their big yummy breakfasts) or to a restaurant that serves seafood and steak.

Anyone who's close to Jeff is never surprised if he breaks into song — just like that! Once, after seeing the movie *Ghost*, Jeff started singing "Unchained Melody" to his date. She thought he sounded terrible (how wrong she was!) and even suggested he never sing again! It really bummed him out, but Jeff didn't let her opinion stop him from going after his dream. Good thing, too, because 98° might have never gotten together.

As much as Jeff is considered the joker of the group and makes the other three guys crack up, he also likes it when people make *him* laugh now and again.

Music is a big part of Jeff's life, and one of his favorite love songs is "It's So Hard to Say Good-bye to Yesterday," by Boyz II Men. He also likes his own group's "Still." Though he's a singing superstar, Jeff considers himself a regular guy.

This regular guy is also a pretty generous guy. Though he rarely lavishes gifts on himself, he bought his mom a Mercedes, his dad a motorcycle, and his girl-friend a truck. And you can bet his daughter has a roomful of teddy bears and toys! This Taurus has a big, big heart.

Chapter 6

They Write the Songs

The Power of Voice

98° is certainly in a position to hire the most talented songwriters in the world, so what's stopping them? Unlike a lot of other bands and singers, it's really important for 98° to write their own songs. As a singing group, Jeff, Justin, Nick, and Drew's chief instruments are their voices. Their strength lies in their harmonies, not in some wild riffs, cool dance moves, or slick designer duds. For their voices to really shine, the guys need to make contact. That means they've gotta connect with the words. Then the emotion follows, and the fans start swoonin' with their croonin'.

It's a fact that lots of singers sound so good because their voices are pumped up and down with the aid of computers. But not 98°! The quartet possesses something a lot of groups lack — *fantastic* voices.

Partly, it's something they were born with. And partly, the guys put in a lot of hard work from day one. They honed their vocals skills in talent shows, and in the beginning, nothing was too small. After working daytime odd jobs to support themselves, Justin, Nick, Drew, and Jeff spent long nights practicing vocally, just as a rock band would practice playing their instruments. All that hard work gave the guys a solid foundation.

Pure and silky vocals are something the guys still very much believe in. When they appeared on TV's *The View*, one of the other guests that day, Dean Cain (he played Superman on the television series *Lois & Clark*), told an interesting behind-the-scenes story about 98°. Before Dean was due in front of the camera, he was hanging out backstage. He spotted Drew, Nick, Justin, and Jeff harmonizing. Dean was so in awe of the foursome's voices, that he stood there, mesmerized.

You can bet when 98° came out a little later to sing "Give Me Just One Night *(Una Noche)*," their voices were in perfect tune and sounded just dynamite — thanks to their practice-makes-perfect performance.

The Power of Love

Have you ever wondered what it takes to write a heartfelt ballad à la 98°? A lot!

There's no set formula for writing a song, and the guys have expressed in past interviews that the process varies from song to song. Some seem to "write themselves," and others require a little more coaxing, a little more patience.

For the tunes on *Revelation*, the guys did whatever worked. Some lyrics they wrote together, and others they wrote alone. More often than not, they started with an emotional theme and built the lyrics around it.

But for four individuals to sit down and agree on the wording of a song (much less a whole album!) is no easy task. How do they do it?

Sometimes the guys pair off. "Stay the Night" and "Yesterday's Letter" were cowritten by Drew. Drew also had a hand in "Dizzy," along with Rhett Lawrence. The final track, "Never Giving Up," was cowritten by Jeff and Justin.

Still, as a song is being fleshed out, the guys make sure they don't dis the other members. They continue working together and look to each other for suggestions, guidance, and help. For instance, though his little bro cowrote "Dizzy," Nick was responsible for penning the rap. There was a blank space in the song, and Nick decided to fill it in. He thought up a rhyme and started doing a rap. "It was something fun to do," he said.

In the end, who came up with which line in which song doesn't matter to the guys. As long as the songs are strong and they're feeling the emotion when they're singing them, they're happy.

The same goes for who ends up singing lead vocals on a song. Nick and Jeff have sung a lot of lead vocals in the past, but now Justin and Drew are singing some leads as well. Nothing is written in stone — they just try to do what feels comfortable as a group as well as what will make the song come alive.

Of course, it's a major plus that the quartet shares one common bond (other than all hailing from Ohio): Jeff, Nick, Drew, and Justin just love girls and dig being romantic. So the warm fuzzies in their songs tend to blossom right from their hearts. And all those tender feelings soon follow, gushing out in their smooth-as-silk lyrics.

The Power of Truth

Something that 98° has been clear about from the start is staying honest. In the beginning, they were pressured to say they were younger than they really were, but the guys wouldn't go for it. "We decided that honesty would be the best policy," Jeff tells.

It's not much different when it comes to their songwriting. Their songs aren't about any one girl, with the exception of Nick's tribute to Jessica in "My Everything."

Still, 98° songs have the magical power of speaking to every girl, young and old alike. If you didn't know, the guys have a huge fan following not only in the United States but also in Europe, Asia, and Australia. One of the big reasons why the super positive message of 98° songs is so well received around the world is because the language of love is universal.

Have you ever felt like one of 98°'s songs was written just for you? Or maybe you're convinced Jeff, Nick, Justin, and Drew are reading your mind when it comes to matters of the heart?

Well, you are definitely not alone. There are plenty of 98° fans who feel the exact same way. That's how the guys know they're succeeding — if you're feeling what they're feeling when they're crooning a song onstage, then that to them is one of the hugest compliments.

Since the guys are so inspired by love and romance, lots of times you can see their own personal heartaches and triumphs wound into both the ballads and the upbeat tracks on *Revelation*. That intense honesty is what unites their hearts with the hearts of their fans.

There's no doubt about it — Justin, Nick, Jeff, and Drew put their true souls into every song.

Pen a Tune

Now that you know a little something about how Nick, Jeff, Drew, and Justin go about writing a song, why don't you try writing a song for them? Go for it!

_____

_____

_____

_____

_____

_____

_____

_____

_____

_____

_____

_____

_____

_____

Chapter 7

Burnin' Up the Charts

Jeff, Justin, Nick, and Drew are not newbies when it comes to chart-topping success. Their 1999 holiday album, *This Christmas*, peaked at number 27 — out of 200 — on the *Billboard* charts, while *98° And Rising* climbed to number 14. On the *Billboard* Hot 100 charts, "Because of You" hit number 3, "The Hardest Thing" hit number 5, and "I Do (Cherish You)" hit number 13.

So it was business as usual when *Revelation* hit the charts at number 2 its first week out. Rapper Mystikal nabbed the number one slot that week. To get the number 2 position, 98° sold more than 276,000 copies of *Revelation* the week of its debut. That's nothing to sneeze at . . . especially when the singer you knocked down to number 3 was none other than the diva Madonna!

Britney Spears also couldn't take the heat. The guys shattered Brit's record for most-added top 40 radio single. Oops! Sorry, Brit. Her "Oops! . . . I Did It Again" was added to 155 top 40 stations in one week, while 98°'s first single, "Give Me Just One Night (*Una Noche*)" was added to *170* stations in a given week. That's 170 adds out of a possible 172. Pretty impressive, wouldn't you say?

Music Is an Adventure

The guys of 98° dig all kinds of music, especially those rooted in heavy harmony and romance (like their own!). *Revelation* is proof of their far-reaching tastes. It's a slammin' mix of roots and flavors.

Along with the classic Motown sounds, the foursome grooves on rock, funk, hip-hop, soul, R&B, Latin, gospel, and many, many other styles of music. In fact, collecting CDs is a passion of all four guys, and they're constantly sharing "fave songs" with each other.

Some of the stars and bands that the guys cite as major faves include Stevie Wonder, Boyz II Men, Take 6, George Clinton and Funkadelic, James Brown, Prince, Seal, Lenny Kravitz, Michael Jackson, and loads of classic Motown singing groups. Nick even digs the harder sounds of Metallica and Guns 'N Roses. The list is long, and the guys keep adding to it every day.

And their own music is only made edgier by their varied tastes.

"I think we were starting to get classified as strictly a ballad group, and we never wanted that," Drew told *USA Today*.

Speakin' Spanish

Even though none of the guys speaks Spanish fluently, they didn't let that stop them from recording "Give Me Just One Night (*Una Noche*)." Working with a language pro on the pronunciation of the Spanish words helped a lot. They practiced until the Spanish-laced love song flowed easily from their lips.

When "*Una Noche*" came out in late summer 2000, a lot of fans scrambled for their Spanish dictionaries to try to figure out what the lyrics whispered by a mysterious female voice at the end of the song meant.

Some fans grilled the guys during an online interview about the meanings of words. "It's basically something like, you're so hot and I love the way you move, the way you touch me . . . yadda, yadda," Nick explained.

"Really passionate" is how the guys have described

the song, and they're not kidding. They don't call themselves 98° for nothing.

FYI: Justin fell in love with the language, and he decided to take Spanish lessons sometime soon. It's actually one of his goals for 2001.

Is Justin's goal inspiring you to learn a foreign language this year, too?

It's just another plus of being a 98° fan — their music and excitement about living life to the fullest just may inspire you!

A Hint of Hip-Hop

If you remember, while putting together their second album, *98° And Rising*, one of the producing teams the quartet teamed up with was the Trackmasters. In the past, the Trackmasters had worked with superstars such as Mariah Carey, LL Cool J, Will Smith, and Mary J. Blige. If you've ever given the above artists a listen, then you know that their musical styles span a wide range — from emotional ballads to rap, from hip-hop pop to urban R&B.

So the hip-hop flavor on *Revelation*'s "Dizzy" is not so far out for 98°. Although Nick, Drew, Jeff, and Justin wouldn't describe themselves as hip-hop singers much less *rappers*, they do dig some hip-hop. In fact,

Nick's CD collection includes the raps of Dr. Dre and Notorious B.I.G.

A style will find its way into their own — naturally and honestly. That's what happened when Nick started rappin' on "Dizzy." His bandmates and the producers thought it sounded awesome, and the rap ended up in the song. Of course, Nick thinks it's pretty neat, too.

Sometimes the group is turned on to something new by one of the producers they've decided to team up with for a particular song or project. Sometimes they're struck by an oldie but goodie. It all depends on what sounds right and moves them at the time.

How adventurous! Not knowing exactly where a song or album might lead them is what keeps making music so fun for 98°. Challenges, excitement, new directions — it's what it's all about!

If 98° fans are willing to taste new music treats, then Jeff, Nick, Drew, and Justin are ready to cook 'em up! They're willing to go searching for hidden treasures and share them with you. Are you ready to come along for the ride?

Chapter 8
Making Fanz Dizzy

What is it that makes girls "dizzy" at the mere mention of the name 98°? A lot of fans would tell you that the first and foremost thing is the group's music. Jeff, Nick, Justin, and Drew would be happy to hear that. They've never really wanted to be remembered for how cool their clothes looked or that really neat spin they did during their stage show. All that stuff is great, but their music should be their legacy.

Don't get them wrong. Every one of the four cuties melts when girls shout "I love you!" to them onstage or when they're making an appearance.

Jeff said in an online chat: "It's very flattering."

Aside from the music, what are some things that make fanz dizzy about Nick, Justin, Drew, and Jeff? Let's take a look.

Physically Speaking

The guys are hunks with a capital H. With Nick's precious smile, Jeff's buff bod, Drew's dreamy eyes, and Justin's classy moustache and goatee, it's no wonder girls all over the world scream with delight whenever 98° takes the stage. And scream and scream and . . .

Funky Style

If there's another thing that all 98° fans will agree on, it's that the guys all have a great sense of style.

What is style? It's a whole lot more than what kind of outfit a person wears. Style is artistic expression. It stems from things like the clothes you're drawn to, the way you talk, the foods and flavors you prefer to eat, the scents you dig, and the sounds you enjoy hearing.

And then there's the element of style that's harder to define — vibe. It's the invisible rays of attraction. They work kind of like a magnet, drawing you closer and closer to a person. When you like someone's vibe, then it's fair to say you dig 'em.

One of the main vibes of 98° is to stay positive and know the importance of love. But individually, what is it that you like the most about each 98° honey? What is it that you like about his funky style? His vibe? A lot, huh? Here are just a few of those things.

As a young child, Justin dreamed of being a rock star someday. He was fashion forward and loved the designs of Polo clothing. Today, he still thinks Polo offers some great styles for the male wardrobe, and hey, he's a music star, too. Some of Justin's other fave designers include Ralph Lauren and DKNY. One thing that he enjoys collecting is sunglasses. He's got oodles of shades in his shack!

Sometimes Justin likes coloring his hair. If you remember, not too long ago he dyed his brown hair blond. Now Justin is back to his natural brown. What hair color did you like better on Justin?

While Justin collects sunglasses, Drew collects baseball hats. Surely you've seen this cutie in one of his trademark baseball caps. He likes to wear them forward and backward, but mostly turned around. Better to look into his dreamy hazel eyes that way. Drew is a sporty guy, and he prefers the sporty, ready-to-go style of designer Tommy Hilfiger.

Nick and Jeff like the urban chic of Phat Farm clothing and a bunch of other designers. They like comfy clothes, but they also like to dress up. Have you ever seen them in a tie? Whew! They look pretty sharp.

It isn't news to any 98° fan that the guys are also into tattoos. Drew and Nick share a similar tattoo design. It's a band around the arm sporting the initial L for Lachey. They got their armbands back in 1996 at an Atlanta tattoo parlor to symbolize their closeness as brothers. FYI: Drew's armband tattoo is a little bigger than Nick's.

Nick also has two other tatts — the 98° sun and a tribal one on his back. The one on his back, which he describes as a Phoenix, took about an hour for the tattoo artist to complete. "It symbolizes rebirth and determination," he shared in an online chat room.

Jeff has four tattoos — the 98° tatt and three that he describes as being very spiritual in nature. Two of the three are in Japanese and translate to "heaven" and "luck." The fourth one, which is on his back, he keeps secret. It's the one that is most special to him.

If you've ever gotten within sniffin' distance of these sweeties, then you know that they smell scrumptious. What kind of cologne works that magic? Drew says he prefers Allure for men, while Jeff dabs on a little Armani when he's in the mood. And Nick? He keeps it natural and doesn't often wear cologne. Justin lets his mood decide his scent.

What About You?

How would you describe your style/vibe?

1. _____
2. _____
3. _____
4. _____
5. _____

Muscles and Manners

Though their schedules are packed to the max, it's obvious by their booming biceps and triceps and everything else that these guys definitely *do* make time for the gym. Jeff follows a strict diet and also lifts weights. He's always been pretty buff, though. The positions he's played in football are inside linebacker and defensive end (read: big and brawny). Did you know Jeff's original career choice was to be a pro and play in the National Football League? It's true.

Another way the guys get exercise (aside from dancing during their shows) is by playing sports. Justin prefers kicking around a soccer ball. Nick runs and lifts weights to keep fit. He also shoots hoops with bro Drew. The Lachey brothers used to play a lot of b-ball when they were growing up. Nick even admits he admires his little bro's hook shot.

Sports were so important to Nick that when he went off to Miami University in Ohio, he decided to pursue a degree in sports medicine. To this day, Nick still loves sports, and he counts those times he got to meet his sports idols as being among his fave memories.

In fact, if Nick weren't in a singing group, he'd most likely be doing a job connected with sports. He wouldn't mind being a sports anchor on the news or maybe a commentator during games.

If you remember, Nick got to portray a boxer in the video for "The Hardest Thing." It's one of his favorite videos because he says it helped him to get into shape. Plus, he really loved working with director Wayne Isham.

ESPN is Nick's favorite TV station, and if he's logged on to the Internet, he makes a point of checking into ESPN.com where he gets the scoop on his favorite teams and sports stats.

Jeff, who isn't exactly lacking in the muscles department, worked as a security guard when he first moved to Los Angeles. He and Justin worked as guards at several rock clubs on the Sunset Strip. Jeff also worked as a night guard at a residence. The lucky client? Singer Phil Collins's ex-wife. Jeff worked from eight at night until eight in the morning walking around her estate to make sure everything was secure.

But as buff as the guys are, their great bods are only part of their hunk appeal. Another plus they have going for them is their good manners. In Polo, Hilfiger, or Phat Farm, onstage or in the studio, at home or on the road, Nick, Drew, Justin, and Jeff are super polite. Holding doors for ladies is the norm for this sweet four-some. They're perfect gentlemen and Midwestern to the core.

Where did they learn such good manners? Well, surely their parents had something to do with it. And Drew got a little help from the army. He joined the re-serves in 1994 (that's where he received some of his emergency medic training).

Also, the pace of life in Ohio where all the guys are from can be laid-back and charming. Drew thinks Mid-westerners are generally more polite than folks are in other parts of the country. And that Midwestern polite-ness has definitely rubbed off on all four of them.

Nick, Jeff, Justin, and Drew very much believe in treating others as they would like to be treated —

with respect. Something they do to keep themselves grounded is check one another. And if one of them is down? Well, then the other three get busy trying to get that guy's spirits up.

Before 98° is a group, they are family. Since the start, they've grown together like brothers. Or, as they'd say, they've definitely got one another's backs.

How They Play

So what do the guys do for fun? Well they're definitely tight, and they do hang out together a lot in their free time. As you already know, they really love to get a good dose of sports. Justin said a while back that the guys are all football fanatics, and if there's any way they can re-arrange their schedule so they can see a game, they do it!

In addition to football and soccer, Justin also plays tennis. He doesn't mind hitting the video arcades now and again, either. Virtual reality games are his favorites. You might also find this laid-back honey grooving at a jazz club. Some of his fave jazz artists include Sarah Vaughan and Ella Fitzgerald. He also has fun shooting pool with his friends back in Cincinnati.

Though Justin says that he finds something special about every country that they've visited while on tour, he's really liked Indonesia, Australia, and Italy. In the

United States, he loves vacationing in Santa Fe, New Mexico.

Sweetie pie Drew loves to get away from it all by going camping. He's definitely not squeamish around bugs, but bears? That's another story! When he wants things to be a bit more warm 'n' cozy, Drew heads off to a cabin in the mountains.

Nick's free time lately is almost always spent with his true love, Jessica Simpson. He spends a lot of time trying to catch up with her on the phone. Nick likes the calm pace of Ohio but also enjoys vacationing in Florida, Hawaii, and Colombia. When he's back in Cincinnati, he likes going to the latest movies with pals and eating Skyline chili. Actually, when the guys go back to Ohio, it's sometimes the first place they hit! What is Skyline chili? Unlike chili that eats like a meal or "Texas-style" chili, this Cincinnati-style chili is more of a topping and is often poured over hot dogs and spaghetti.

Jeff hangs out in Southern California where he has a house. Much of his free time is taken up writing songs. He does, however, find time to add to his massive football card collection. (He has thousands of cards!) He also enjoys reading, and one of his all-time favorites is *The Alchemist* by Paulo Coelho.

As far as traveling is concerned, Jeff's at home everywhere. On tour, he likes to soak up the sun in places like Australia and Southeast Asia. He also likes to vacation in Panama City, Florida.

It's All Good

When Nick and Jessica Simpson started dating more than two years ago, they took a good long while to decide if they should let the cat out of the bag. Eventually, they decided that it would be better to let the world in on their romance. Being honest is very important to both of them, and they didn't want to sneak around. Quite the opposite, actually. Nick and Jessica wanted to shout their love for each other from the mountaintops.

Once they let people know they were dating, Nick and Jessica received lots of letters of support from fans. "That means the world to me that people look at us and see how in love we are and see us as an inspiration," Nick told *Teen People*. They both feel they have some of the best fans in the world.

Upon their "revelation" that they were dating, Nick and Jessica also received lots of interest from the press. Privacy is a thing of the past for this super-hot couple. Still, they don't regret their decision. The truth is, if they were dating or not, both Nick and Jessica would still be getting plenty of attention because of their superstar status.

Even when they're not working, the guys in 98° get recognized a lot. Their private lives are very public. Ever since they formed in 1995, the spotlight has rarely been off the group for very long. Even when the guys head off on vacation, there are not many places Jeff, Nick, Justin, and Drew can go without getting mobbed by fans and photographers. Sometimes, fans by the hundreds turn up at the airports awaiting the foursome's arrival.

It comes with the territory, and they know that. They won't lie: They occasionally do miss being able to do ordinary things such as wandering through a mall. But reaching people through their songs is very important to them. And meeting fans and doing photo shoots and signing autographs are all part of the joy of making music. They feel very honored to be living out their dreams and touching so many lives. They feel blessed to have so many loyal fans.

Still, it makes you wonder how their lady loves handle all the attention the guys get. Do they ever get jealous? They've learned that it's just part of the business. They also know that, though the guys sing love songs to thousands of fans, in the end, their hearts belong to them.

"We're the lucky ones," said Drew of their romantic relationships on the talk show *The View*.

What are some things that make you "dizzy" about 98°?

1. _____

2. _____

3. _____

4. _____

5. _____

Chapter 9

On the Road Again

When you hear someone say a band is "on the road," it means the group is in transit or traveling between gigs or appearances. As you already know, in an effort to reach their beloved fans, 98° does an awful lot of hopping on and off planes. They can be in two or three cities on any given day. Sure, it's a lot of fun to travel, but it's no wonder that once in a while one of the guys gets a little "dizzy" and forgets exactly which city he's in.

Want to know what might happen in a typical day for 98° while they're on the road? Let's go!

Video Venture

If Nick, Justin, Jeff, and Drew aren't in the studio recording songs, there's a good chance they're on the road. A good portion of their traveling is done when they perform at concert venues all over the world and attend press conferences. And sometimes they have to travel to go on location when they're making music videos for songs.

Often, the video for the first single from a new album is shot before the album actually drops. That's how it worked with the first *Revelation* single, "Give Me Just One Night (*Una Noche*)."

For that video, the guys worked with director Wayne Isham (he did the last three of the group's videos as well as the video for Will Smith's "Miami"). The quartet is a huge fan of Wayne's work and totally trusted him with his vision for the video. When he closed his eyes and imagined the guys crooning "*Una Noche*" in the exotic location of Mexico, the guys packed their bags, pronto! (If you've caught the video on TV, you know the location was just perfect for the song.)

Wayne created a whole fiesta-type set with a Day of the Dead Parade (celebrated throughout Mexico on November 1 and 2 to honor the souls of the dead, who are believed to return to be merry and celebrate with living relatives). That might explain the mysterious woman who appears and disappears in the hauntingly beautiful video.

Most of the video was shot on the site of Mayan ruins in Mexico. One of the cities the guys visited during the shoot was Chichén Itzá, or "Mouth of the Wells of Itzá."

The Mayan ruins are absolutely stunning, and when Drew, Justin, Nick, and Jeff first arrived on location, the scenery took their breath away. According to Justin, they were "incredible locations."

It might sound like the guys went on *vacation* rather than location, but video shoots are actually more work than play. In fact, for hours and hours of shooting, roughly only a minute or so gets into the final version. The rest ends up on the cutting room floor. There are lots of takes, and the guys have to sing — and act — from their heart each and every time.

According to Nick, there were some long, hard, hot days. Not only that, but there were also a few unwelcome visitors.

"Lots of bugs!" Nick said in an online chat.

But after all the hard work, Nick was pretty pleased. "We couldn't have asked for more," he said of the whole experience.

Meet the Press and Fans

After the video was done, the guys were whisked off on a massive publicity tour to get the news out — 98° was back with a brand-new album!

The best way to do this is to go from state to state. If you live in a small town and wonder why the guys usually stick with the bigger cities when it comes to making in-store appearances, it's because they want to reach a lot of people at one time.

Not that Nick, Drew, Justin, and Jeff wouldn't want to hit each and every town in every state and country. They love being on the road. But if they did that, you wouldn't be seeing their fifth album anytime soon. They'd be too busy traveling.

A publicity tour often includes meeting with the press. During the actual recording of an album, a group or singer may be holed up in a studio for months and months, so when they finally get a chance to talk about what happened in there, you can bet they're excited. This is the time when the public gets to hear a lot of the details about the actual recording process, the stories behind the songs, and the group's hopes for the album.

Since 98° loves to perform and the guys are so devoted to reaching out to their fans across the world, in addition to talking to the press they performed "Give Me Just One Night, (*Una Noche*)" on a lot of talk shows (one even from the rooftop of CNN).

They visited radio stations, too, and dropped by record stores and performed for thousands of fans at places like the Mall of America in Bloomington, Minnesota.

Expect the Unexpected

As you've probably guessed, the group's schedule is pretty tight, organized down to the hour and sometimes the minute.

Occasionally, something unexpected happens, such as a plane delay or a traffic jam or some other problem, and everything is thrown off track. The guys are pretty good-natured and flexible when they have to hang tough and wait for things to get back on schedule.

That's what happened with the special concert they filmed for the Disney Channel.

Did you happen to catch the concert Nick, Drew, Justin, and Jeff taped especially for the Disney Channel back in October 2000? The show was taped in Ohio, and though a good part of their time was to be spent working, the guys were totally psyched about being back in their home state.

After arriving, the band prepped for the show and got pumped up thinking about the mega-welcome they'd get from their hometown fans. Before they could go on stage, though, they got another kind of *roaring* welcome. A bad storm blew in through Cincinnati and wrecked part of the stage.

The concert and taping had to be bumped back a few days. Though the guys had no control over the weather, they still were bummed. They felt badly about all the fans they had let down since many people had marked their calendars for that special day.

But when it finally came time for them to get the show on the road, the wait seemed to make everything sweeter for both the group and the audience. The guys were amazed by the loyalty of their fans. A lot of them stuck it out, waiting hours and hours just so they could see 98° perform.

And the loving fans? They got to see a touching, heartfelt performance of a lifetime. Good thing the Disney Channel got it on tape!

Looking back, the guys were pretty happy with the way things turned out. Though the fans had to wait and the group's schedule was thrown off a bit, they did get to spend some extra time in their native Ohio. You can bet they had a blast.

And Then There's This

In between all the press appointments and performances, the guys stayed busy. They had to squeeze in rehearsals with the troupe of talented musicians and dancers who accompany them during their *Revelation* tour. The guys had to get comfortable with the new show and dance moves. (If you've already caught the guys on the *Revelation* tour, then you know their 2001 show is packed with lots of fancy footwork.)

If you think the day is over after an exhausting rehearsal, forget about it. You know those gorgeous pin-ups fans collect? They come from photo shoots, and Jeff, Drew, Nick, and Justin know how important they are. That's why they make time to pose for those sometimes tedious sessions, which include wardrobe fitting and makeup. (Yes, guys do wear cover-up stuff when needed.)

Then, the guys might have an online chat on the Internet scheduled. They love doing online chats because it's a cool way to reach a lot of fans from all over the world in an up-close-and-personal way. It's nice to be able to answer questions the fans have directly. And the fans love it because they get immediate replies.

If they have some extra time in the day, Jeff, Nick, Justin, and Drew try to squeeze in a workout at the gym and, um, oh, yeah, eat some food. Can't forget to eat!

Speaking of food, the group prefers simple over fancy any day. They're definitely meat-and-potatoes guys. Forget the finger sandwiches — pass the burgers, fries, and pizza, please.

By the time the official appointments are over, it can be very late. Still, the band has other commitments to fulfill, such as returning phone calls, catching up with family and loved ones, and answering some fan mail.

When it comes time to go night-night, sometimes sleep doesn't come easily, even though they're wiped out.

Their minds might be racing with the day's events and all the people they've met. Occasionally, as with the time they got to hang out with Stevie Wonder during a video shoot, they feel like it's all a dream.

But it's not, of course. It's a dream come true!

Added to the thrills of meeting rock stars, celebs, sports stars, and other people they admire are the challenges of having to sleep in strange hotel beds and cramped plane seats, adapt to different foods and time changes while in foreign countries, and stick to tight schedules. A lot of times, the guys don't get very much sleep. It's easy to see how life on the road takes some getting used to.

But don't think 98° is complaining. They wouldn't trade their lives for the world. One look at their fans and the guys wake right up. Nick says he gets a lot of his energy from the excitement and love of 98° fans.

And soon enough, Jeff, Justin, Nick, and Drew are sleeping snugly in their beds, dreaming sweet dreams.

Back on the Bus

If the guys are lucky, they might get a few days off to catch their breath and nab a few winks. But they usually can't get too comfy because soon after the interviews and photo shoots, it's time to hit the road for a different focus — a worldwide concert tour. Many lucky fans have shared this awesome experience with the guys, no doubt.

Touring is something that goes hand in hand with putting out a new record, and the guys look forward to it. They really enjoy meeting all their fans and having an opportunity to thank them in person for their support. "We love performing live," Drew once said in an interview.

What to Pack?

There are some things that the guys always bring with them when they're traveling. They try not to overpack or bring too many extras because they know they have to schlepp their stuff from city to city. That's why traveling light is the only way to go.

The guys are great pals and keep each other entertained while traveling by telling jokes (Jeff keeps them laughing!) and talking about how a show went and how they can make it better.

Sometimes, even with Jeff's jokes, it can still get a little boring on the tour bus or plane. To help pass the time, the guys watch movies and play video games. Madden Football is one of their favorites.

Two other on-the-road necessities for Jeff, Drew, Justin, and Nick are their CD players and laptop computers.

Jeff takes it one step further and usually brings along a 16-track digital workstation so he can write and do production on the road. He loves writing songs.

Drew always brings a camera and takes mostly black-and-white shots. He likes to document the group's experiences on the road. Who wouldn't want a peek at *that* photo album?

Justin often packs a nonfiction book to read and a journal where he can jot down his and the group's experiences.

Nick brings his favorite CDs. He's always on top of

the latest releases. One of his faves is, of course, *Sweet Kisses* by Jessica Simpson!

There's no doubt that life on the road can hold all sorts of excitement, from bumping into other singers and celebrities to experiencing unexpected delays to spur-of-the-moment performances. If you were to go on the road with 98°, what are some of the things that you would absolutely positively take with you? Here's a checklist for your treasures. . . .

1. _____
2. _____
3. _____
4. _____
5. _____
6. _____
7. _____
8. _____
9. _____
10. _____

Missing You

The guys have adapted pretty well to what Nick once referred to as the "migrant existence." When they're on the road, they can be away from home for months and sometimes years. They end up missing family and friends — a lot. Who do they miss the most when they're feeling homesick?

Nick

Nick misses his family and, of course, Jessica. Since she's also busy touring and promoting her music, a lot of their time is spent catching up on the phone. You can bet both of them are thrilled when their career paths cross and they get to perform or make an appearance together at a music event. When Nick has time off, that doesn't necessarily mean Jessica does, so what's the solution? Nick sometimes travels with Jessica during her tour just so they can spend some time together.

Drew

Though Drew has big bro Nick along for the ride, he still misses his family and his new bride, Lea (if she's not on the road with him as one of the dancers). He also misses being able to take off in his SUV to a nice remote locale and camp out.

Justin

Justin misses his family and hometown friends a lot. "When I go back home to Ohio, I like to hang out with my friends, shoot pool, and check out local bands," he says. He also misses Skyline chili like crazy (so do the other guys). Good thing for Justin that the company offers a Skyline Crave Kit that he can order through their Web site and have shipped to him wherever he is on the road.

Jeff

Jeff also misses his family and girlfriend. He respects them and is so grateful that they stand behind his decision to be part of a singing group. Another thing he misses is kicking back and watching a good football game. Since his career keeps him so busy, he rarely gets to see a complete game. And that's pretty tough for a guy who used to be glued to the set every weekend!

Chapter 10

The *Revelation* Tour

Loving Every Minute

As much as the guys miss being back in Ohio with family and friends, they really do love touring because it gives them a chance to connect with their fans. And that's way important to them.

Though Drew says touring and being in the studio both have their pros and cons, he really looks forward to getting out there and seeing the fans. He lives for live performances.

"My favorite part is seeing the fans react to our songs and seeing them sing along," said Jeff during an online interview.

And connect they do. There are plenty of 98° fans who will tell you how amazing it is to be at one of their concerts — gazing into Nick, Jeff, Drew, and Justin's eyes as they croon one of their dreamy love songs and singing right along with each beautiful word.

Girls and guys alike (yes, there are a lot of guys who look up to the group, too) just love to sing along. From the band's point of view, it's really neat to look out into the crowd and see people connecting emotionally through the words and music. 98° and their fans feel the power!

Concerts are also cool because the group feels the music in a different way when they perform it live. They can add extra parts to a song, and they also feed off the crowd's sizzling energy and excitement. And that makes it more relaxed for Nick, Justin, Drew, and Jeff.

Not that the guys don't have a tight show. Have you seen some of their moves? Now, they've never claimed to be dancers, but you've got to admit they can groove onstage. And during the *Revelation* tour, fans are out of their seats gettin' jiggy, too.

Ever wonder if 98° gets the jitters before *they* get jiggy? For sure, Drew admits. But he considers this a good thing — it keeps him on his toes!

One thing that helps to prepare 98° for a performance is that before each show, the guys warm up their vocal cords by going through a series of voice exercises in different scales.

Another way they rev up before a show is that Nick, Justin, Drew, and Jeff make a point of getting together in a huddle and counting their blessings. They feel very honored to be sharing their gift of voice with the world, and they don't want to take any of that for granted. Huddling up and praying also helps them clear their heads and stay focused for the upcoming performance.

Even though the guys are hitting many cities when they're on tour, they feel each one is different and special. They give their all at each and every performance, and each show ends up being as unique as their songs.

Don't Miss the Fab Four

If you haven't seen 98° on the *Revelation* tour yet, psych yourself up for an explosive show with excellent music, awesome dancing, and a flaming pyrotechnics (fireworks) show that's leaving audiences stunned.

The guys knew the up-tempo tracks on *Revelation* would call for some up-tempo moves. And boy, oh, boy, do they deliver — 98° style!

Hot vocals. Hot tunes. Hot outfits. Hot bods. Hot moves. Hot musicians. Hot dancers. Hot light shows.

Nick has described the show in two simple words: "High energy!"

You can bet no one's sitting down when the group belts out the super-hot "Give Me Just One Night (*Una Noche*)," the funky fresh "Dizzy," the groovin' "The Way You Want Me To," and the soulful "You Should Be Mine."

When the guys slow things down with one of their trademark ballads such as "My Everything," "Always You & I," "The Way You Do," and "Yesterday's Letter," the whole audience starts swooning. "You Don't Know," which speaks of the heartache of life and love, is full of emotion and tenderness. Though Nick, Drew, Justin, and Jeff sound great on their album, the live experience is really something else — just amazing. Their vocals weave together so perfectly it leaves fans totally breathless.

Justin, Nick, Jeff, and Drew pride themselves on their powerful voices, and in person, their a cappella harmonies are intensely beautiful.

On *Revelation*, the a cappella interlude "I'll Give It All" is a sparkling gem. When the guys sing it live, it sends shivers down many a spine. In fact, some fans were a little disappointed that there weren't more interludes like "I'll Give It All" on *Revelation*.

Don't worry. The guys haven't forgotten about their strength as a cappella singers. They're still huge fans of Take 6 and other a cappella harmony groups. In the future, they hope to do more a cappella singing. So keep an ear out. Each 98° concert is different, and you never know when the guys will throw in some vintage harmonies from their earlier days.

Girls lucky enough to be near the stage will sometimes throw roses at the feet of their fave guy. Some fans have four roses — one for each hunk.

There are some neat surprises, too. In the past the guys have been known to do some covers of fave tunes at their concerts. During their last tour, they did a version of "Superstition," which was a huge hit for Stevie Wonder. Some fans loved the 98° cover so much that they wanted the guys to record it and put it on a future album. Ya never know what 98° will do next!

Sometimes after a show, the guys kick back by meeting fans and contest winners. It amazes them how dedicated their fans are — taking time to run their own 98° fan clubs and Web sites and traveling great distances to catch them on tour.

Everybody Say "Oops"

Ever wonder if the guys ever had some stage, um, trouble? Of course they have. They are human, you know.

Once Jeff was walking backward onstage while singing to a female fan when he tripped and fell. The microphone sailed into the crowd, and yes, people laughed. Good thing he has a great sense of humor!

Another time, Drew hit Jeff in the face — accidentally, of course!

Then there was the time Nick's overalls came down onstage. He caught them just in time and continued right along with the show.

In another clothing crisis, Justin once split his pants onstage. He also kept right on going, but not without getting hysterical first!

In fact, all the guys find their boo-boos pretty funny. That doesn't make the moments so mortifying, does it? A sense of humor definitely helps.

Chapter 11

All-Around Act

When Hollywood came knocking, you can bet Nick, Drew, Jeff, and Justin were ready. Shortly after wrapping production in Mexico on the video for "Give Me Just One Night (*Una Noche*)," the cuties headed north into the heart of Hollywood, California, to film an episode of the television comedy series *Just Shoot Me*.

The episode was titled "A Night at the Plaza" and aired on October 19, 2000, on NBC. The guys guest-starred as members of 2 Fine, a band put together by *Blush* magazine's Finch (played by David Spade). When Finch's boss Jack (played by George Segal), is heartbroken, Finch convinces 2 Fine to perform to try to cheer him up. Naturally, Jack is moved by the fluttering Spanish guitars and hypnotic vocals of "*Una Noche*" and ends up feeling much, much better.

If you happened to catch the "A Night at the Plaza"

episode of *Just Shoot Me*, then you know that the quartet is pretty comfortable in front of the cameras. If they ever decide they want to give acting a go, they surely have promising new careers ahead of them. In fact, one member of the group is no stranger to acting at all.

When Jeff moved to Los Angeles to go after a career in entertainment, he landed several acting jobs (including a U.S. Navy commercial). Though Jeff enjoyed acting, he decided music was his first love. That's when he began focusing his energy on putting together a singing group. Soon enough, 98° was born, and their urban R&B songs started climbing the charts.

Even after 98° was off and running, Jeff wasn't completely cut off from acting. He could have his cake and eat it, too, so to speak, because the group began getting invitations to appear on popular television programs. In addition to appearing on *Just Shoot Me*, the guys have appeared on the daytime soap opera *As the World Turns* and the sitcom *City Guys*.

And though Nick has said how much he admires actor Bruce Willis and that he thinks it would be cool to be in Bruce's shoes for a day, it doesn't look like the guys will be leaving music for show biz anytime soon. Shortly before *Revelation* was due out, the guys were asked if there was a chance they would make a movie soon. Their reply was a firm no. Drew said their plates are pretty full with making their records. "We feel if we're going to do something, we should give it 100 percent."

Looks like Drew, Jeff, Nick, and Justin are all having way too much fun making beautiful music together and heating up the stage during their worldwide *Revelation* tour!

Chapter 12

Didn't You Know?

Some Top Honors

1. 98° taped an awesome special concert for the Disney Channel back in Cincinnati around the same time *Revelation* was released in 2000. Another guest on the special was Hawaiian sensation Hoku.

2. Some of the many top talk shows the guys have appeared on include *The Rosie O'Donnell Show, Live With Regis,* NBC's *Today Show,* MTV's *Total Request Live,* and *The View.* How many of these shows did you catch?

3. Drew, Justin, Jeff, and Nick performed "Give Me Just One Night (*Una Noche*)" for the first time on the *Teen Choice Awards* in August 2000.

4. Some of the charities 98° have worked with and have supported in the past include the Race to Erase

MS (multiple sclerosis), the Pediatric AIDS Foundation, the Make a Wish Foundation, Habitat for Humanity, and the "Reggie Bowl." They especially enjoy helping charities that benefit young people.

5. In 2000, 98° performed at Arthur Ashe Kids' Day and helped to officially kick off the U.S. Open. The event benefited the USA Tennis National Junior League, a program that was founded by tennis great Arthur Ashe to offer opportunities in tennis to disadvantaged youths.

6. The hot foursome made hearts flutter when they performed at the *Miss Teen USA Pageant* in August 2000.

7. Nick and Jessica performed their duet single "Where You Are" at special screenings of the film *Here on Earth,* starring Leelee Sobieski and Chris Klein.

8. The quartet rang in the new millennium by performing on MTV's *New Year's Eve Bash* on December 31, 1999.

9. 98° was asked to sing the national anthem during game five of the Chicago Bulls/Utah Jazz Game, a Superbowl halftime event, and at Dodgers Stadium. You can bet these four sports lovers were thrilled!

10. At the 1999 *Billboard Awards*, 98° was nominated in the Duo/Group Artist category. The guys were in great company. Other nominees in that category were Sugar Ray, TLC, and the Backstreet Boys.

Chapter 13

Awesome Memories . . .

1. The guys count the time when they got to meet Stevie Wonder and perform their duet "True to Your Heart" on *The Tonight Show* with the superstar as one of their most memorable experiences.

2. Christmas is a special time for the guys, and you can bet they said yes when they were asked to participate in the Christmas tree lighting gala at Rockefeller Center in New York City in 2000. The special was televised on NBC, and the 20 thousand lights strung all around the plaza were an unforgettable sight.

3. Jeff, Justin, Nick, and Drew have fond memories of the time they got to spend with Mariah Carey. They had all looked up to her as a singer for a long time, and when they got to finally meet and sing "Thank God I Found You" with her, it was a dream come true.

4. Another great memory is when the guys got to meet President Clinton. They were invited to the White House to perform for a special, *Christmas in Washington*, in 1999.

5. Hitting a few balls during batting practice with the Cincinnati Reds was quite memorable for 98°. And hanging out at the Cincinnati Bengals' training camp in 2000 sure was fun, too!

6. Jeff had to overcome his fear of heights when filming the video for "Because of You." If you remember, the guys crooned the tune from atop the Golden Gate Bridge in San Francisco, California. He says standing so close to the sky is something he will always remember!

7. One great memory for the guys is when "Because of You" broke the top 10. They were psyched!

8. The very first time the guys heard their music on the radio is a special memory. They were at a hotel, and they fell completely silent listening to the song. It took a moment to sink in, but then they went crazy, jumping for joy.

9. The guys will never forget a couple of fans who went to extremes to meet them. One fan flew all the way from the Czech Republic to meet them during an in-store appearance. Another time, a girl actually jumped out from under a catering cart and started taking pho-

tos of the group. Needless to say, they were surprised and very much flattered.

What are some of your most memorable moments of 98°? Jot them down here.

1. _____
2. _____
3. _____
4. _____
5. _____

Chapter 14

Backtrackin'

98° Discography

Albums

98°, Motown Records, 1997
Note: There are two versions of the debut album. After *98°* was released in 1997, the guys recorded "Was It Something I Didn't Say" by Diane Warren and decided to reissue *98°* with the new song in 1998. They replaced "You Are Everything" with "Was It Something I Didn't Say."
98° And Rising, Motown Records, 1998
This Christmas, Universal Records, 1999
Revelation, Universal Records, 2000

Singles

"Invisible Man"
"Because of You"

"The Hardest Thing"
"I Do (Cherish You)"
"This Gift"
"Give Me Just One Night (*Una Noche*)"
"My Everything"

Music Videos

The group has made music videos for the following songs:
"Invisible Man"
"Was It Something I Didn't Say"
"True to Your Heart"
"Because of You"
"The Hardest Thing"
"I Do (Cherish You)"
"This Gift"
"Give Me Just One Night (*Una Noche*)"
"My Everything"

Songs Recorded with Other Artists

"True to My Heart" with Stevie Wonder, appears on the *Mulan* soundtrack.

"Thank God I Found You" with Mariah Carey, appears on the diva's album *Rainbow*.

The duet "Where You Are," which Nick recorded with girlfriend Jessica Simpson, appears on her album *Sweet Kisses*.

Soundtracks

The *Mulan* soundtrack features "True to My Heart."

The soundtrack for the film *Notting Hill* starring Julia Roberts features "I Do (Cherish You)."

"The Love That You've Been Looking For," a 98° original song penned by Nick and performed beautifully by the group, appears on the soundtrack for the CBS miniseries *Jesus*. Some of the other performers included on the soundtrack are Hootie and the Blowfish and Lee Ann Rimes.

The Nick Lachey and Jessica Simpson duet "Where You Are" also appears on the soundtrack for the film *Here on Earth*.

"Fly With Me" appears on the soundtrack to *Pokemon The First Movie*. Britney Spears, Christina Aguilera, and 'N Sync also have songs on this album.

Video

Heat It Up: The Video

Chapter 15

Hot Fax to the Max

    1. Nick and Jeff didn't study Spanish in high school. They took French.

    2. The group signed their first record deal on April 8, 1996, with Motown Records.

    3. When Drew was four years old, he was afraid Jaws (the scary shark from Steven Spielberg's movie *Jaws*) was going to come and eat him up.

    4. The guys did a Spanish version of "Give Me Just One Night (*Una Noche*)."

    5. There are two versions of "This Gift," which appears on *This Christmas*. The second one that appears on the holiday album is a pop version.

    6. "I Wanna Love You Forever" is Nick's fave Jessica Simpson song.

    7. Justin has described the guys in 98° in the fol-

lowing way: Jeff is the joker, Nick is the most intense, Drew is sarcastic. And himself? Laid-back.

8. When the guys first moved out to Los Angeles, they had a tough time getting dates.

9. The girl featured in the video for "Give Me Just One Night (*Una Noche*)" is Joyce Giraud. She was Miss Puerto Rico in the 1998 Miss Universe Pageant and nabbed second runner-up.

10. There's a stunning, sizzling, stupendous official 98° 16-month calendar with exclusive pics offered through the 98° official Web site. Get 'em while they're hot!

11. Drew is big on adventure sports, and one thing he would love to do is skydiving.

12. Nick's favorite ice cream flavor is pistachio.

13. "I Do (Cherish You)" was originally recorded by Mark Wills and topped the country charts in the summer of 1998.

14. On January 27, 2000, the group's second album, *98° And Rising*, went platinum for the fourth time over.

15. One of Jeff's favorite movies is *The Shawshank Redemption*, starring Tim Robbins and Morgan Freeman.

16. Justin's favorite all-time role model is Stevie

Wonder. Some of his favorite Stevie songs include "Superstition," "Lately," and "Ribbon in the Sky."

17. Though the guys don't play instruments on their albums or onstage, they can each play different instruments. Nick can play the saxophone, Jeff can play the trumpet, Justin can play the trombone, and Drew can play percussion.

18. Tito Puente, an amazing jazz musician and composer, was scheduled to be a special guest percussionist on "Give Me Just One Night (*Una Noche*)." But sadly, right before he was due in the studio to work with the guys, Mr. Puente became ill and passed away. The guys were deeply saddened and felt the world of music had lost a great legend.

19. Drew is a hero! Several times, he's come to the rescue and lent a hand to people who were in distress. One time on a plane, he helped a woman who was having a seizure. His experience as an emergency medical technician came in really handy. (He had that job in New York before he hooked up with 98°.)

20. The bride in the "I Do (Cherish You)" video is played by 1996 Miss USA, Ali Landry.

21. Jeff once worked in a Chinese restaurant as a cook and busboy, and Nick was a delivery boy for a Chinese restaurant.

22. More than 1500 fans showed up to see 98° perform at the Mall of America in October 2000.

23. Originally, the guys were supposed to do the song "True to Your Heart" from the *Mulan* soundtrack with the Temptations instead of Stevie Wonder.

24. When they need to quench their thirst, each guy grabs something different. Drew likes lemonade, Nick likes Yoo-hoo, Justin likes OJ, and Jeff just likes something cold and refreshing.

25. Once, a Malaysian fan gave the guys turtles as a gift.

26. Drew and Nick's mom, Cate, is a huge Stevie Wonder fan.

Chapter 16
The Way You Want Them

Fan Dos and Don'ts

The guys think 98° fans are the best in the world. If you consider yourself their number one fan, you probably know all these things already, but for some of us who don't, remember these fan dos and don'ts.

As a 98° fan, what should you *do*?

1. Definitely *do* make a lot of noise whenever you see the guys in concert. It lets 'em know you're out there.

2. Definitely *do* keep writing those fan letters. Nick said that they really do try to read every single one. Even his grandmother helps!

3. Definitely *do* try to grow with them as a group —

both musically and artistically. It's *you* who keeps them movin' forward.

What should you *not do* as a fan of 98°?

1. Definitely *do not* pounce on the guys and scream loudly in their ears. They won't be able to hear your questions and your words of love.

2. Definitely *do not* believe the rumors. The guys try not to pay attention to them, and you shouldn't, either.

3. Definitely *do not* sit in your seat if you feel like dancing at their concerts. One of the main reasons the guys made a point of including upbeat tracks on *Revelation* was to get people dancing. So get up and do your thing!

If fans everywhere keep the faith and love strong, then you can bet the ride with 98° will be filled with great music, hidden surprises, and lots of fun.

Logging On

Needless to say, getting some downtime is like getting a present for these cuties. They like staying busy and are totally devoted to their fans. It's important to them that their positive message about the power of love reach as many people as possible.

A long time ago, before they were popular, the guys made a pact among themselves to try to give back as often as they can to their fans and the community. Adoring fans like you are what make 98°'s success so sweet.

That's why the sweeties often make time for online chats through sites such as America Online, MSN, and MTV. Even when they were smack in the middle of recording *Revelation*, they took time out to log on to their computers and chat with their adoring fans.

Now that you know about the group's fondness for talking with fans on the Internet, don't you think you should be prepared? You never know when you'll bump into Jeff, Justin, Drew, and Nick in a chat room, so use the space below to jot down some of those super important questions.

Online questions for Nick

1. _____
2. _____
3. _____
4. _____
5. _____

Online questions for Jeff

1. _____
2. _____
3. _____
4. _____
5. _____

Online questions for Justin

1. _____
2. _____
3. _____
4. _____
5. _____

Online questions for Drew

1. _____
2. _____
3. _____
4. _____
5. _____

Show Them You Care

Since Nick, Drew, Justin, and Jeff have been touring for months and are so far from home, now is the time to show them that you care. If you can't get to one of their concerts, you can show your support in lots of other ways.

Start by pouring your heart out on their personal message board at their official Web site. The guys put a lot of time and effort into keeping the Web site fresh, and it's got the latest scoop on what's up with the band. Often, there are links to other Web sites featuring info and interviews with the band as well as a feature called On the Spot where each member answers personal questions posted by fans just like you. Through the official site, you can also participate in important polls to let the guys know where you stand, and you can even send a good chum of yours an awesome 98° e-greeting card. Pretty neat, huh?

Stayin' in Touch Online

Log on to the 98° official Web site at **www.98degrees. com**.

For the official 98° fan club, log on to the 98° official Web site above and click on Fan Club. Don't forget there's an annual membership fee to get the perks of being an official fan club member, so be sure to ask your parents for permission first.

Log on to the Universal Records official Web site at **www.universalrecords.com**.

Some other cool web sites that have covered 98° in the past are:

www.mtv.com
www.billboard.com
www.cdnow.com

Stayin' in Touch by Mail

If you want to write to these old-fashioned sweethearts the old-fashioned way, by sending a handwritten love letter, here's the 98° official fan mail address:

98°
P.O. Box 31379
Cincinnati, OH 45231
USA

Chapter 17

The Third Degree On 98°

Test your 98° knowledge by answering these 16 questions. If your brain has soaked up all the info in this book, you'll ace the quiz 'cause the answers lie in the book. *And* the 16 answers are printed on the pages following the quiz. Good luck!

True or False
1. **Drew, Justin, Nick, and Jeff always write song lyrics together.**
2. **Drew really likes to be called Andy.**
3. **When the guys first came to Los Angeles, it was hard for them to meet girls and date.**
4. **Nick goes gaga for action movies like *Die Hard*.**
5. **Though some of the lyrics for "Give Me Just**

One Night (*Una Noche*)" are in Spanish, none of the guys speak Spanish fluently.

6. Jeff, Drew, Justin, and Nick cowrote most of the songs on *Revelation*.

7. The title of 98°'s 1999 Christmas album is *The Gift*.

8. "I Do (Cherish You)" was featured on the soundtrack for Disney's *Mulan*.

9. Before he hooked up with the other guys to form 98°, Justin was a paramedic in New York.

10. Nick, Drew, Jeff, and Justin are all from Kansas.

11. The video for "Give Me Just One Night (*Una Noche*)" was filmed in Japan.

12. The guys crooned to President Clinton at the White House as part of Christmas in Washington in 1999.

13. On *Revelation*, Drew raps on the track "Dizzy."

14. One of Justin's nicknames is Droopy.

15. After seeing the movie *Ghost*, Jeff sang "Unchained Melody" to his date, and she told him he sounded terrible.

16. Nick's fave ice cream flavor is chocolate.

THE THIRD DEGREE ON 98° ANSWERS

1. False

Sometimes they write separately and then compare notes.

2. False

Though Drew's full name is Andrew John Lachey, he prefers to be called Drew and not Andy. Calling him Andy is "a complete no-no."

3. True

Believe it or not, the guys didn't have girlfriends when they first moved to LA.

4. True

Nick's favorite movie is *Die Hard*, starring Bruce Willis.

5. True

Though the guys learned the pronunciation of the Spanish words in "Una Noche," none of them are fluent in Spanish.

6. True

The group cowrote 11 of *Revelation's* 13 tracks.

7. False

The title of 98°'s 1999 Christmas album is *This Christmas*.

8. False

"I Do (Cherish You)" was featured on the soundtrack for the film *Notting Hill*, starring Julia Roberts.

9. False

It was Drew who was working as a medical technician in New York before he joined 98°.

10. False

All four members are from Ohio.

11. False

The video for "Give Me Just One Night (*Una Noche*)" was filmed in Mexico.

12. True

Their performance at the White House made it a memorable Christmas.

13. False

Nick raps on "Dizzy."

14. True

In addition to Droopy, another one of Justin's nicknames is Hydro.

15. True

Boy, how wrong Jeff's date was — she's probably kicking herself right about now, don't you think?

16. False

Nick's fave ice cream flavor is pistachio.

Can't get enough of your favorite rock, pop, R & B, and Hip-Hop stars?

Check out
Celebrity Quiz-o-rama #2:
MUSIC MANIA!

❓ Break this code to find out Aaliyah's real name: LLWTJLS

❓ 98° plus A*Teen plus TLC = how many people?

Strut your stuff with crosswords, secret codes, word searches, brain-teasers, and more all about your favorite music makers and shakers. Rack up Pop Points along the way to find the chart topper among all your friends!

POP TO IT!